Can a Giraffe Cry or Laugh?

Mary Elizabeth Salzmann

Consulting Editor, Diane Craig, M.A./Reading Specialist

ABDO Publishing Company

Published by ABDO Publishing Company, 4940 Viking Drive, Edina, Minnesota 55435.

Copyright © 2007 by Abdo Consulting Group, Inc. International copyrights reserved in all countries.

Printed in the United States.

Credits
Edited by: Pam Price
Curriculum Coordinator: Nancy Tuminelly
Cover and Interior Design and Production: Mighty Media
Photo Credits: BananaStock Ltd., Digital Vision, Eyewire Images, JupiterImages Corporation, ShutterStock, Stockbyte, Stockdisc, Wewerka Photography

Library of Congress Cataloging-in-Publication Data
Salzmann, Mary Elizabeth, 1968-
  Can a giraffe cry or laugh? / Mary Elizabeth Salzmann.
      p. cm. -- (Antonyms)
  ISBN-13: 978-1-59928-714-0
  ISBN-10: 1-59928-714-5
  1. English language--Synonyms and antonyms--Juvenile literature. I. Title.
  PE1591.S25 2007
  428.1--dc22
                            2006032021

SandCastle™ books are created by a professional team of educators, reading specialists, and content developers around five essential components—phonemic awareness, phonics, vocabulary, text comprehension, and fluency—to assist young readers as they develop reading skills and strategies and increase their general knowledge. All books are written, reviewed, and leveled for guided reading, early reading intervention, and Accelerated Reader® programs for use in shared, guided, and independent reading and writing activities to support a balanced approach to literacy instruction.

Let Us Know

SandCastle would like to hear your stories about reading this book. What is your favorite page? Was there something hard that you needed help with? Share the ups and downs of learning to read. We want to hear from you! To get posted on the ABDO Publishing Company Web site, send us e-mail at:

sandcastle@abdopublishing.com

SandCastle Level: Transitional

Antonyms are words that have opposite meanings.

Here is a good way to remember what an antonym is:

antonym
=
opposite

Also, **antonym** and **opposite** both start with vowels.

3

antonyms

Joey is crying because he hurt his hand.

antonyms

Alexis is laughing because she is having fun with her friends.

antonyms

Taylor gets bored on long trips.

antonyms

Sammy is excited because it is his birthday.

antonyms

Christian is being rude when he sticks out his tongue.

antonyms

Vicky is being polite when she raises her hand before speaking in class.

antonyms

These friends are jumping around
and acting silly.

antonyms

Benjamin is serious when he does his homework.

antonyms

Austin loves orange juice, but he hates grapefruit juice.

antonyms

Sydney was sad, but then her friend Megan cheered her up. Now Sydney is happy.

antonyms

Logan is tired. He will get a good night's sleep so he will be alert in school tomorrow.

antonyms

Rachel was upset by a bad dream. She told her mom about it, and now she is calm.

Antonym Activity

bored   excited

cry   laugh

polite   rude

alert   tired

20

Antonym Pairs

alert — tired

bored — excited

calm — upset

cry — laugh

happy — sad

hate — love

polite — rude

serious — silly

In each box on page 20, choose the antonym that describes the picture.

21

Words I Know

Nouns
A noun is a person, place, or thing.

birthday, 7

class, 9

dream, 19

friend(s), 5, 10, 15

fun, 5

grapefruit juice, 13

hand, 4, 9

homework, 11

mom, 19

night, 17

orange juice, 13

school, 17

sleep, 17

tongue, 8

trips, 6

Adjectives
An adjective describes something.

alert, 17

bad, 19

bored, 6

calm, 19

excited, 7

good, 17

happy, 15

her, 5, 9, 15, 19

his, 4, 7, 8, 11

long, 6

polite, 9

rude, 8

sad, 15

serious, 11

silly, 10

these, 10

tired, 17

upset, 19

Words I Know

Verbs
A verb is an action or being word.

acting, 10
are, 10
be(ing), 8, 9, 17
cheered, 15
crying, 4
does, 11
get, 17
gets, 6

hates, 13
having, 5
hurt, 4
is, 4, 5, 7, 8, 9, 11,
   15, 17, 19
jumping, 10
laughing, 5
loves, 13

raises, 9
speaking, 9
sticks, 8
told, 19
was, 15, 19
will, 17

Proper Nouns
A proper noun is the name of a person, place, or thing.

Alexis, 5
Austin, 13
Benjamin, 11
Christian, 8

Joey, 4
Logan, 17
Megan, 15
Rachel, 19

Sammy, 7
Sydney, 15
Taylor, 6
Vicky, 9

About SandCastle™

A professional team of educators, reading specialists, and content developers created the SandCastle™ series to support young readers as they develop reading skills and strategies and increase their general knowledge. The SandCastle™ series has four levels that correspond to early literacy development in young children. The levels are provided to help teachers and parents select appropriate books for young readers.

Emerging Readers
(no flags)

Beginning Readers
(1 flag)

Transitional Readers
(2 flags)

Fluent Readers
(3 flags)

These levels are meant only as a guide. All levels are subject to change.

To see a complete list of SandCastle™ books and other nonfiction titles from ABDO Publishing Company, visit www.abdopublishing.com or contact us at: 4940 Viking Drive, Edina, Minnesota 55435 • 1-800-800-1312 • fax: 1-952-831-1632